YELLOW WEDNESDAY

by Jimmy Black

*The gathered bric-a-brac of living in Glasgow ......
and in places measured from Glasgow.*

Illustrations by Catherine Neville

Glasgow District Libraries 1988

To Betty,
Sally Anne, Gary, Caroline,
Gordon, Sarah and Callum.

ISBN 0-906169-23-2

Published by Glasgow District Libraries,
The Mitchell Library, North Street, Glasgow G3 7DN.

Typeset by Newtext Composition Ltd.,
72 Waterloo Street, Glasgow G2 7DA

Printed by Bell & Bain Ltd.,
303 Burnfield Road, Thornliebank,
Glasgow G46 7UQ.

CONTENTS

FOREWORD

What a daft title for a book, eh!? Yellow Wednesday. And it's got nothing to do with eating bananas or scrambled eggs in the middle of the week – even though I've enjoyed both, quite often, on Wednesdays.

The title is caused by the chemistry of my mind: an odds-and-sods concoction distilled from conditions . . . influences . . . events . . . places . . . people . . . Well, I was born left-handed. On the First of April. In Manchester. Two Glaswegians – my father and mother – just happened to be there at the time.

She sang silly songs. He told terrible tales. And they brought me up in Glasgow among characters, some of whom would have made Damon Runyon's ears curl. They took me to cinemas, churches, museums, markets, theatres, libraries, football grounds, carnivals, parks, music halls, all to make sure I got well sprinkled with the city's magic powder.

And in an otherwise unremarkable schooling, there were unforgettable teachers. Jonah Graham . . . Miss Forbes . . . Teuchter Matheson . . . Daddy Sinclair. They all tried sticking life's facts into my head and managed to get some of life's fancies in as well.

By this time, my imagination had become so severely infected that I was writing verse which actually got printed in the Gossip and Grumbles column of the Glasgow Evening Times. More contaminations got into my day-dreams when I went to learn the brick-laying. There was no escape from characters like "Speak-a-Meenit" and "Chantie-Mooth".

So many of the people who rubbed against me through those years, elbowed their way into my script-writing for BBC radio and for Scottish Television. And now they've gate-crashed this book.

Oh, the title? Yellow Wednesday? Well, you see, since my earliest days, for me, Monday, Tuesday, Wednesday, Thursday, Friday, Saturday and Sunday have never been just big dods of time. Each has its own special colour. Seven colours so vivid I put them into rhyme. So. Yellow Wednesday.

Jimmy Black.

GLASGOW

Unmatched for gettin' oot the rut,
Oor city wins the coconut . . .
But, even when it's in a habble,
Oor city is inimitable!

UP OUR CLOSE

Our old tenement stair was a vertical village. Weren't they all? People living under and over each other, somehow had to get on with each other. We mostly did, somehow. Coalmen, milkmen, paper-boys and such, identified each storey as "Wan Up", "Two Up" and "Three Up". On each landing, the room-and-kitchen nearer the head of the stair was referred to as "The Furst" ...... the single-end in the middle was called "The Middle", and the room-and-kitchen further from the head of the stair was known as "The Faur-away".

When the boss coalman said to his mate, "Two bags o' nuts – Three Up – The Faur-away", the coal-carrier knew he was doing the furthest, highest climb up the close – top landing – far-away door – and twice! A hundredweight at a time!

We never really got annoyed with John (Wan Up – The Furst) as he thumped his way through his piano lessons as if he were wearing boxing gloves . . . and we just laughed at big Andy (Two Up – The Faur-away) bouncing drunk off the close walls and serenading his wife, as he always did . . . "You may not be an angel . . . For angels are so few . . . But until the day that one comes along . . . I'll string along with you . . . Hic . . ."

And what could we have done without Mrs Kennedy (Three Up – The Furst) who nursed the sick . . . laid out the dead . . . and who took weans by the ankles at the moment of birth and skelped their backsides to welcome them into the world . . . Or Willie (Three Up-The Middle) who cleared choked jawboxes, climbed ronepipes and breached kitchen windows to open doors for harassed wives who had locked themselves out . . . Willie who always told us next summer would be a scorcher . . . Living up a Glasgow close had more often to be endured than enjoyed . . . away back then . . . but those people put the music, the smells and the colours into it that made it bearable . . .

DAY COLOURS

Here, think o' the days o' the week – can you find
The colours they offer the eye o' the mind?
See, Monday's as blue as the deep o' the sea . . .
Yet, Tuesday's as rusty as buildin'-site tea . . .
An' Wednesday's yellow – like butter on breid . . .
Oh, Thursday . . . slate-gray . . . like the minister's heid . . .
Ah, Friday's as rid as the big barmaid's lips . . .
Then, Seturday's tawny – like sauce on your chips!
Noo, Sunday, of coorse, has nae colour at a' –
Aye, Sunday is whiter than Christmas cerd snaw . . .
So, you can see nane o' my colours? Oh, well,
Take next week – start paintin' the days for yoursel' . . .

DRINKING CAPACITY

It was in the days when Tallulah Bankhead was taking baths in champagne and pubs in the Gallowgate were selling beer at a tanner a pint . . . Just after opening time in this pub. A quiet Tuesday morning. Two strangers – definitely not regulars – came in, taking a swing door each. They seemed to be calling each other Jackie and Mickie.

Jackie walked to the low end of the bar where the barman was polishing glasses . . . Mickie walked to the top end of the bar where the boss was working on his books. The barman said to Jackie, "Whit can a get you?" Jackie said, "Waitin' for my mate . . ." Mickie said to the boss, "Can you settle an argument for us? My mate doon there insists that there are four pints in a quart – I say there are only two pints. Who's right?" The boss said, "You are . . ." and put his nose back in his books . . . "Thanks", said Mickie, and went down beside Jackie and the barman . . . The barman said, "Whit are you drinkin'?" Mickie said, "Two pints o' heavy, please." The pints were pulled and placed before Jackie and Mickie . . . The barman said, "A shillin'." Mickie said, "Oh, the boss has jist offered us two pints on the house . . ." . . . and raising his voice . . . "Isn't that right, boss? Two pints!" The boss shouted back, "Aye . . . two pints . . ." Without taking his nose back out his books . . . Jackie and Mickie drank their pints without putting a shilling across the counter. Of course, they were never regulars . . . Definitely not regulars.

WAN NIGHT O' LOVE

Eliza Plugg wis plump an' sweet,
A nicer lass you couldny meet ....
Sae feart an' shy o' nips an' squeezes,
But light an' warm as summer breezes .....
For years, I tried, withoot success,
Wi' a' the tricks o' style an' dress ....
An' then – at last I reached my aim –
Eliza let me see her hame!
The night wis daurk .... we walked thegither ....
Her eyes were starin' at each ither ....
Her mooth wis ... delicately sma'?
A scarlet gash frae jaw tae jaw!
Her dress, sae neat at bust an'hip,
Reminded me o' Celtic's strip ....
Her hair displayed a yellow rose
That matched the snotter at her nose!
We reached her cottage on the hill,
An' losh! the night got daurker still! ....
Unbridled love I longed ta gi'e her –
But, damn it a'! I couldny see her!
I stood wi' neither light nor staur,
As somethin' thudded in the glaur –
I staggered roon' wi' slides an' slips –
Then, Precious Joy! I found her lips!
That sloppy mooth began manoeuvres ....
An' sooked like half-a-dizen Hoovers!
But sense an' time frae me were gone ....
So kiss for kiss I gi'ed till dawn!
I greeted daylight's early traces
Wi tattered collar ... tie ... an' braces ....
Farewell tae sweet, romantic night!
Then, jings! I saw a dreadfu' sight!
Eliza Plugg, the silly bitch,
Wis lyin' smoothered in the ditch ....
An' there, I'd coorted a' night through –
A Cathkin fermer's big, broon coo!!!

WELL, NOT EVERY BOAT IS A DREAM BOAT!

It's perhaps slightly un-nerving to think that it was a series of wee twists and turns of Fate which determined whether or not you would ever come into this world – that is – you – the unique product of two people!

Well, I know for sure that on a summer holiday Monday early this century, the prospect of existence for me hung in the balance.

You see, that was the day Sarah Palmer agreed to go on a date with big Cherlie Laird who lived up the next stair. He offered to take her on a day trip – sailing all the way from the Broomielaw to Rothesay and back. Sarah said yes. They took the tram to Broomielaw. Cherlie got two three-ha'penny tickets. Aboard the "Lord of the Isles", Cherlie paid the fares.

The sail down the river was pleasant, but two or three times, Cherlie excused himself and slipped away down a stair. It was when he returned for the third time that Sarah noticed just a fine trace of white powder round his lips. Soon, he was away again – indeed, his disappearances became so frequent Sarah suspected he either had a weak bladder or was taking medicine for heartburn ..... When he slid off for the ninth time, she decided to shadow him .... And in a wee passageway near the engines, she saw him stop .... turn his face in towards a corner, take a big paper bag from his overcoat, take a handful of yon powdery marshamallow sweeties out of the poke and stuff the lot into his wide-open gob!

This episode created some disquiet in Sarah's mind ..... She got even more concerned .... because they had got as far as Dunoon and Cherlie hadn't even asked her if she fancied a cup of tea – far less a marshmallow!

Imagine the state she was in getting off the steamer at Rothesay ..... staggering with hunger and thirst .... deprived of .... tea .... a biscuit .... even a powdery sweetie ..... They walked along the prom towards Ardbeg .... and Sarah was saying to herself in desperation ... "He's takin' me tae wan o' the top class hotels for a slap-up lunch ..... No? ..... tae wan o' the restaurants on the front for a pie an' beans ..... No?..... Oh, please God .... make him take me for a poke o' chips!" That particular prayer was not answered. Cherlie was for buying her nothing!

Just ahead of going into a coma, Sarah made the excuse of going to find a ladies' room. She rushed up a side street into a dairy – got two doughnuts and a half pint of milk, and guzzled the lot as fast as she could swallow! Later, she had to work the same trick to get a cup of tea at the pier tearoom.

Of course, Cherlie too, was still doing his "excuse me" bit ... and Sarah reflected later that she was sure his voluminous overcoat concealed not just marshmallows, but a flask of tea and slices of bread with cold steak and onions jammed between them! She swore she could smell the onions on his breath! And there were crumbs of bread in the powder round his lips ... On the sail back up the Clyde, Cherlie and Sarah actually managed to have snatches of conversation without once using any embarassing words like "soup" ... "tattie scone" .... or "fritters" .... And not one teaspoonful of sustenance did he invite her to partake of .....!

Back home in the room-and-kitchen in Westmuir Street, Sarah gave her mother a stomach-witness account of her day of fasting. Old Mrs Palmer was fuming!

She cried, "Never bought ye as much as a cup o' tea the hale day?' The meanjie sod! Ah'll blacken his name a' through the steamie! Here! Awa' up an' shame the big eejit! Take your tram fare and your boat fare up tae his door right noo – an' slap the money in his face!"

Sarah took to the idea. Up she went with the precise amount to Cherlie's door. He opened it and she said, "Cherlie, here's my tram an' boat fares for the day – I wouldny like you to be short o' money for marshmallows ...."

Cherlie kind of quivered ... and said, "Sarah! You did not need to come to this door this night with this money ..... it wid hiv done at the end o' the week ..... " ....!

As that day ended, Sarah reckoned her future really belonged – not with Cherlie – but with big Jimmy who lived up the end close .... And it did. They were the only two people who could have produced me.

Marshmallows? Well, I can take them or leave them .....

QUEUEING FOR ALL PARTS

No city could boast a richer variety of cinemas than Glasgow. It offered the lot – from the "crooked-pinkie" tea-drinking of La Scala in Sauchiehall Street to the leg-numbing balcony seats of Tollcross Cinema. There was the heady, mystical, magical perfume of the Palaceum in Shettleston .... a subtle blend of the smells of orange peel .... thick-black tobacco smoke ... gas-light fumes .... and the sickly disinfectant spray an attendant squirted over you three or four times during a performance .... And there was the breath-taking spectacle of the windmill on the Seamore Cinema up Maryhill Road ...

But I reserve a special place in memory for the Black Cat which was just the flash of an usherette's torch away from Parkhead Cross. The building is still there. It's a film studio now. Once, it was a BBC studio, but it's heyday was when the best of Hollywood was flickered down that long, stark, rectangular auditorium ... which was never really built to show talking pictures.

It wasn't just the fact that I saw the film, "Flying Down To Rio" in the Black Cat that made the place unforgettable for me – even though "Flying Down To Rio" starred Dolores Del Rio and Gene Raymond, with a supporting act of two hoofers called Ginger Rogers and Fred Astaire. No, it wasn't just that.

What made the Black Cat unique was that it had a resident flea called "Big Rosie". "Big Rosie" was revered throughout the district. Indeed, it was considered a mark of honour about Parkhead to be bitten by her.

Many a strong man, standing drinking pints in a local pub, would pull up his sleeve .... proudly to reveal a line of fiery lumps on his forearm .... And admiring mates would gasp in awe, "Big Rosie!?" The man, with a break in his voice, would reply, "Big Rosie ...."

Dear knows how many generations of fleas "Big Rosie" begat, but she was at the Black Cat for a long time .... After she was found dead in the cheap seats by a cleaner one Monday morning, there was a ceremonial cremating of her remains in the boiler-house fire .... at which, the manager was heard to intone, "Goodbye, Big Rosie ..... we shall never be bitten by your like again ...."

No other city had cinemas like the Glasgow cinemas .....

THE KING DID HIS LEVEL BEST

What a splendiferous occasion it was on the 14th of May, 1903, when King Edward the Seventh gathered with all the dignitaries of Glasgow Corporation at the corner of George Street and Montrose Street in Glasgow .... The King was to lay the foundation stone of the Royal Technical College (which in half-a-century or so would become the University of Strathclyde). A wide circle of proud workmen .... joiners ... masons .... bricklayers .... navvies .... formed the periphery of this historic scene .... One of those working faces in that ring belonged to a lad who some seventeen years later would become my Father .... He was an apprentice bricklayer with the builders – the great P. and W. Anderson Limited. And my future dad was dressed in his fresh white moleskin overalls .... World War .... General Strike .... Hunger Marches .... would all have come and gone before my dad would tell me about that day at the corner of Montrose Street ....

The foundation stone hung suspended from a block-and-tackle as the builder mason spread the mortar bed that the stone would be set into. At a signal the stone was slowly lowered on to its bed .... The King raised his silver trowel .... tapped it on the four corners of the stone, and said, "I declare this stone well and truly laid ..." In a flash, the foreman mason roared, "Na! Na! Mister King! It's a hair low on this back corner! Up wi' it lads!" Whereupon, the dutiful squad pulled the stone back into the air. History stood still. The highest standards of Scottish craftmanship had to be maintained. The mortar bed was corrected and the stone set level to all the cardinal points. The King fingered his moustache .... and, no doubt, pondered the thought that if a foreman mason could now contradict a King .... was the Empire as safe as it had always been .....?

BEANFEAST

On a Glasgow Fair Monday in my teens, Hughie said to me, "Ever been tae Ayr Races?" I had only seen horse-racing at the pictures, so Hughie said, "Let's go". In our compartment on the train journey from St Enoch's Station to Ayr, we had only one other travelling companion – a fellow who looked like Ramon Navarro, but spoke with the sloppiest Glasgow accent I think I have ever heard. We chatted. Yes, he was going to the races too. Albert, his name was.

But as we got fairly near to Ayr, he revealed that he was not actually going to enjoy the Sport of Kings – he was going on business. We would be about Prestwick when Albert produced a brown make-up substance from a wee bag and proceeded to rub the stuff all over his face and neck! Then, from the same bag he pulled out a multi-coloured scarf and wound it round his head to make the shape of a turban. This completed, Albert took time to explain, "See, lads, whit Ah dae is – get masel' done up like this, then in the station lavvy Ah'll pit oan ma kimono .... Doon at the grocers, Ah'll buy a cupla pun' o' butter beans ..... an' at the track, Ah'll spread them intae ma wee Oriental tray Ah've goat in the bag there .... Then Ah've only goat tae shout tae the punters that Ah've jist received a fresh supply of the lucky, magic beans from ma uncle – Poochara, the sacred man of Delhi .. Ah'll be shoutin' that Ah am Ramha Singh and these lucky magic beans available at the crazy price o' thruppence a time will bestow winner-pickin' powers on any punters that buy them .... But, mind lads, if ye see me – mum's the word – don't blaw me away ....."

Hughie and I were speechless .... we just kind of whistled and drummed the carriage window with our fingers .... But in Ayr, we tailed Albert ..... and sure enough, resplendent in his kimono, he bought two pounds of beans in a grocer's shop ..... I noted the price .... thruppence a pound! And there at the racecourse, we saw Albert going through his performance as Ramha Singh – worthy of an Oscar – and in a rich, "Omar Sharif" accent. He was sold out before the first race ..... I actually bought one of his beans ..... but I didn't have any money to back horses. I gave it to Hughie. Hughie lost his shirt .....

11

MISS CARRUTHERS

So many things changed in the old library. Remember the brackets for the gas mantles on the walls between the windows? They were there even after the war. They disappeared along with the big map of the British Empire .... Oh, yes – and the reading desks with the squiggly legs – they went to make way for the record and cassette shelves. Miss Carruthers never changed, though. Didn't everybody think she had always been there .... and always would be .... Timeless Miss Carruthers! Oh, indeed ..... changeless ..... Twin sets. Hair in plaits. Lemon tea at twenty minutes to eleven .....

Maybe. Sometime. You thought about her. Did she ever take flu' .....? Or fall in love with Clark Gable.....? What would she hum now and again? Ah .... a titbit from "The Mikado". But only at the desk as she date-stamped books .... Hmmm .... "A wandering minstrel, I .... a thing of shreds and patches ..... of ballad songs and snatches ..... and dreamy lullabies ....." She looked not one bit like a wandering minstrel. And never could you think of the neat, precise Miss Carruthers in shreds and patches .... Never. She didn't *walk* about that library. She floated ..... up and down the canyons of books ..... slipping volumes back into their appointed places .....

She was cocooned in soft, warm silence .... and the faintest whiff of her perfume .... was it "Ashes of Roses"? .... It lingered behind her .... until it was overpowered by the odour of the disinfectant lifting from the floor .... The smile too. It was an "always" smile. Offered to anybody. Whether they asked for a copy of "Das Kapital" ... or "No Orchids For Miss Blandish" ..... And there she would go .... ushering the last stragglers out of the reading room ..... and closing the great double doors of the library on the stroke of the clock ..... Those doors didn't even creak ..... They wouldn't have dared ..... And in her astrakhan coat with matching hat, she would go floating off into the blue evening .... through the puddles of amber that pale street lamps spread on the pavement ....

You wouldn't have guessed, would you ...? that, once – Miss Carruthers – stuffed her gym slip inside her knickers and climbed the Academy clock tower for a dare!? Oh, yes she did! She was only in second year, too. The Gazette put her on the front page – knickers and all! Some say the Rector never fully recovered from the shock and the shame! It was never clear, though, which shocked and shamed him more – the mad climb or the public display of underwear! The records say Miss Carruthers was "appropriately punished" ..... Honestly ..... it really did happen .....

What a sensation, too, when she did her Mae West routine at the kirk concert for King George the Fifth's Jubilee! The minister had to leave the hall to compose himself .... and go to the men's room ....!

And don't laugh – this is true! She and Larry won a jitterbug contest in the Isle of Man! Larry .... Yes ..... Larry ..... It did look for a long time, that Larry and Muriel were set to go all the way ahead .... together .... But, they didn't. Oh, the parting wasn't poignant or dramatic. He didn't fall on some foreign field during the war. Oh, no. Larry .... just .... somehow .... faded into the crowd. And Miss Carruthers went on being Miss Carruthers.

There even was – for a time – the ragged nastiness that hinted she had pulled strings to get that job in the library. The only strings Miss Carruthers ever pulled were on a barrage balloon she looked after in her WAAF days – on a site down Brighton way.

It's a few years ago now .... but you must remember. Suddenly, Miss Carruthers wasn't at the library. She had floated off – quietly – into retirement. How could you describe the feeling of finding the library without Miss Carruthers? Like losing a piece from a jigsaw puzzle? No. Like finding a hole in an expensive cashmere jumper? No. It's daft to try putting it into words. But you were in another library now ..... the old one had gone ..... the old one where there had been encounters between "Ashes of Roses" and floor distinfectant.

Miss Carruthers' chair is near the big window up in the long, bright ward ..... on the hill yonder ..... You don't really notice anybody being sad – not really – along that ward ..... The hours are counting away for her. She's resting .... easy ..... happy ..... in a kind of glow of loving care .....

She can't see the library from the big window – not since they built the flats. But she can see the Academy clock tower .... and Lovers' Lane by the playing fields ..... And when she smiles ..... could it be she's listening to echoes .... out of memory .....?

"That girl Carruthers! She's up on the clock tower! Don't move girl! Call the fire brigade .....!

"Ladies and gentlemen! Winners of the star prize in our All-Comers Jitterbug Championship! – from Scotland! – Muriel Carruthers and Larry Mason!!"

"Miss Carruthers! Look at this copy of Palgrave's Golden Treasury! Somebody has stuck chewing-gum in the middle of Tennyson!"

"Red alert!' Raiders over the channel!"

"Oh, we'll meet again, Muriel ....."

"Sure we will, Larry ...."

"Miss Carruthers, do you have a book on the treatment of blackheads .....?"

"Goodnight, Miss Carruthers ..... see you in the morning ....."

WHO'S DEID?

Funerals were spectacular affairs when the ornately-appointed hearses were pulled by shining black horses in splendid mourning livery. The mourners' carriages were also drawn by these magnificent beasts. Any one of them could have been the Red Shadow's cuddy in "The Desert Song". Wee boys like us always did the same thing whenever there was a funeral at one of the closes in our tenement. Maybe it was as a mark of respect to the departed. Anyway, we stopped playing at goodies and baddies and played at funerals instead.

I remember auld McConnell's funeral. Big affair it was. A hearse and six carriages. So Geordie and I crossed our arms behind our backs and gripped hands. We were the horses. Eckie bent down behind us in the "leap frog" position, stretched out his hands and held our arms. He was the hearse. Danny had a rope round our necks as reins. He was the driver. And we made a stately progression up and down the pavement in front of the tenement trying to look like the black, shiny cortege lined up beside us.

On about our second or third lap, an insurance man in a trilby hat grabbed my mate Geordie by the shoulder. He had to be an insurance man to ask such a question. He said to Geordie, "Who's deid, son?" ..... And Geordie said, "How diz the hoarse know ....?!"

THE THING

Commotions often hit oor stair,
An' groans or giggles fill the air.
There was the night when Willie Shaw
Tried oot karate on the wa' .....
He brought his right haun' doon quite hefty,
An' ever since, we've ca'd him "Lefty" .....
Wee spinster Jean, who's ninety-two,
Kicked up an' awfy "how-d'ye-do" .....
An' cried in ecstasy an' pain,
"I think I'm gonny hiv a wean!"
The trouble wis, as you'll hiv guessed –
A feather stuck inside her vest!
But nothin's matched the wild affair
Yon time oor Kate tore up the stair
An' gruntin' like a wounded navvy,
Yelled, "Go an' loack the stairheid lavvy!
I've seen it! An enormous wan!
A monster! Doon the lavvy pan!
It gi'ed me sich a leerin' smile,
It has tae be a crocodile!"
Wee Mrs Platt, across the landin',
Came oot an' roared in wild abandon,
"Aye, Kate, that's true! The thing bit me!
Right on the – stroke o' hauf-past-three!"
The weemin, screamin' at each ither,
Wrung "Fairy Liquid" haun's thegither .....
My mither hit the dug a skelp,
An' chased it oot tae bring some help ....
She moaned, "Who dae you think would bring
This strange, unmentionable thing?
It's them! These weans doonstairs – the gets!
They've jist been gi'ed some funny pets .....
It happened when their silly maws
Took them tae see yon picture, 'JAWS'!
This thing's escaped! Oh, whit a lark!
Defenceless bums bit wi' a shark!
Noo, don't start runnin' holus-bolus!
Keep cool!" Then she cried, "Murder polis!"
The cop who dashed up tae assist,
(As useful as a broken wrist)
Said, "Feed it sleepin' pills in gravy ....

Or – better still – send for the Navy!
An' when we got the Fire Brigade,
A rerr excuse their captain made –
"Aw, naw! This is a tricky wan ....
Oor ladders widny fit the pan!"
As each plan met the cry, "Abort!"
I knew I wis the last resort ....
My mither looked me in the eye,
An' said, "Well, son, it's do or die!
Lift up your courage tae the peaks!
Destroy this thing that's nibblin' cheeks!"
The strain that gripped oor limbs an' faces,
Took a' the stretch right oot my braces ....
Sich times demand mair strength within us ....
So, I knocked back a pint o' Guinness!
Forthwith, I charged, wi' troosers saggin' ....
The wey Saint George attacked his dragon ....
An', lettin' oot a fearsome roar,
I bashed right through the lavvy door!
Wi' hammer raised, I cried for blood!
An' hit the pan a whackin' thud!
It burst in a tremendous shatter!
An' nameless things flew in the scatter!
I knew the creature lay beside me .....
Whit consequences wid betide me?!
"Haud on", I said, an' prayed .... an' hoped ....
Until the snaps an' gurglin' stoaped .....
How could I bring my eyes tae meet
The mess o' debris roon' my feet? .....
I couldny bear tae look at a' .....
Of coorse .... I had tae .... then I saw ....
There .... snarlin' at me underneath .....
My faither's National Health false teeth!!!

THE TRADITION OF THE HOT PO

Sometimes, you may encounter folk who hold to the persistent, though fallacious, belief that the husband of yesteryear was a despot in his own home – that his wife and children were there just to render unto him, slavish service. You'll hear it said that his special chair by the fire .... his reserved seat at the table .... were inviolable! A member of the family would sit on them only if he or she had lost the desire to go on living. Neither wife nor child would dare to speak out of turn .... and food, clothes, paper, pipe, matches .... had to be at his hand at the moment he wanted them. He would speak to his family in snarls .... and that was on *good* days .... when he wasn't swinging the back of his hand at them ....

Well, very, very few of the husbands I ever knew, fitted into that image. By far the great majority of them were loving, caring men who, maybe, on occasion, went "a kennin' wrang", but who dedicated themselves to providing the creature comforts for weans and wife. Such love and care were exemplified in the Tradition of the Hot Po.

Imagine a bitterly cold winter's morning. The temperature up the tenement stair might be verging on freezing point, but in the stairhead lavatory it had plunged to the grimmest, Arctic depths! Now, it was in the natural way of things, that folk waking at five or six o'clock on such a morning, had the desire to relieve themselves of the night's accumulations, but were chilled to the heart by the thought of having to make that sub-zero journey down to the lavvy. It was at such a time that a husband's love and care filled the wee kitchen .....

He would warm a chamber-pot at the kitchen fire .... to take the cold air off it .... and then discreetly slip it under the bedclothes of the set-in bed for his wife's use .. thus saving her from the horrors of catching stairhead hypothermia .... Up our stair, though, there was the legend of Arthur and Elsie. On a cold and frosty morning, Arthur had heated the chamber-pot at the roaring kitchen fire, and had quickly slipped it under the bedclothes for Elsie. Elsie sat on the pot and – instantly – let out an agonising scream which reverberated up and down the stairs of the tenement! Neighbours rushed out of their houses in fright! Yes, you've guessed. Arthur had over-heated the chamber-pot and it had burned into Elsie's tender skin!

The young doctor who responded to Arthur's emergency call was too innocent as yet, to have been tutored in the practices of tenement living ..... But he had heard that certain dermatological diseases were fairly prevalent among the working classes ..... Thus .... when he cast his eyes on Elsie's roasted posterior, he exclaimed, "My God! this is the worst case of ringworm I have ever seen ...."

DECEMBER THE TWENTY-FOURTH

Oh, aye ... the maist magical night o' the year –
Christmas Eve – when auld Santy Claus comes .....
Dispatchin' his presents tae a' the world's hames –
Even hooses that hivny got lums!
It's a mystery yet, how he does it at a' –
Jist as well, of coorse, naebody knows .....
Well, Superman .. Doctor Who ... even star ships
Couldny reach a' the places *he* goes!
As a laddie, I wanted tae *see* Santy Claus .....
So ... at midnight ... I crept doon the stair ....
I quietly opened the big kitchen door ....
An', sure enough, Santy wis there!
He put doon a toty wee flash-lamp for me ....
An' a big boax o' paints for oor Sammy ....
An' then – tae my complete surprise –
He jumped intae bed wi' my mammy!!!

THE CHAMP

What a miserable day it was for sailing down the Clyde. But, there we were – my father, my mother and my brother and me. Wednesday of the Fair week ..... and a steady drizzle. We could hardly see the great hulk of the 534 on the slip-way at Clydebank, it was so misty .... dreich ...

Ah, but the thrill of this trip was that we were on a brand new Clyde pleasure steamer – the Queen Mary! – doing its first season "Doon the Watter"! Little did we know then that our wee boat would become Queen Mary the Second when the 534 became the *big* Queen Mary.

To get away from the ship's band which was playing, "Don't know why ... there's no sun up in the sky ... Stormy weather ..." my father took us to see the engines .... and we really *did* go to see the engines .... Coming along the passageway by the engines were two unremarkable young fellows, except that one was very thin and he had ears like the handles of the Scottish Cup .. My dad said, "See that wee fella wi' the big ears? He's a boxer .... His name is Benny Lynch ...." In little over a year after that boat trip, Benny was universally acclaimed as the Flyweight Champion of the World having beaten Jackie Brown and Small Montana ...

In the mid-thirties, a huge advertisement stretched along the railway bridge over the Clyde. In Jamaica Street. It takes the trains in and out of Central Station. The advertisement proclaimed the virtues of a very well-known wine, and the big slogan which lit up at night said, "SIX AND A HALF POUNDS OF GRAPES IN EVERY BOTTLE!" I thought about that advertisement when I was standing waiting on the terracing at Shawfield Park on a bright summer evening. Benny was due to let the American Jackie Jurich have a go at his world title .... Benny beat Jurich, but it was no title fight .... indeed, Benny had forfeited his title. At the weigh-in .... he had been six and a half pounds over weight ....

Nearly ten years after that summer night, I went with some other lads for a laugh, to the boxing booth on Glasgow Green. The booth was always there during the Fair Carnival .... But there were no laughs .... A fat, sad, sickly-looking wee man sat in one corner of the ring. The crowd stood all round .. The promoter was shouting from the ring ... "Any young fella prepared to try for three rounds with the legendary Benny Lynch?! Come on lads, you'll be able to tell your gran'weans you fought the great Benny Lynch .." Benny still sat in his corner, head down ... as if he were completely indifferent to what was going on ....

One young lad did step up. They took his shirt off and tied on the gloves .. The bell rang ... The young challenger jerked upright and faced the shambling figure coming out of the opposite corner ... bearing not the slightest resemblance to the quicksilver champion of a decade before ... The crowd quietened ... the only noises, the shuffling feet ... heavy breathing ... and the odd slap as the huge gloves met .. Old women in shawls stood round the ringside, their fingers clutching the canvas .... Suddenly the quietness ripped as one of them screamed in a cracked voice, "Gi'e him a tupp'ny wan, Benny!" We were on our way out then ... Just over a year later, Benny died .... He had run out of "tupp'ny wans" .....

WOMEN RULED O.K.

Wasn't it always the mothers and grannies, the big sisters and aunties ...
the womenfolk ... who set the rules of respectability and behaviour to
be observed by all, without exception, who lived up your tenement
stair? The roster for stair-washing, lavvy-washing, use of the back-court
wash-house, determination of the quality of pipeclay to be used for stair
bordering, the restriction of games of wee heiders to the rear end of the
back close .... and only on very wet days! These were the regulations

administered by a committee of the women – a committee that never met and never disbanded ..... never wrote down a single rule ..... The women conveyed their requirements by whisper, yell and withering look .... Persistent rule-breakers quivered in repentance under a wrath blasted at them with "Genghis Khan" intensity.

But it was those women, too, who taught us the rules for using the stairheid lavvy down on the half-landing. Rules based on the edict that you must never ever give anyone outside the family, the slightest hint that you ever actually used that stairheid lavvy. You had never to be seen going to or coming from that place! This was achieved by the application of a technique passed on from generation to generation. It operated thus.

On requiring to "go", you collected the lavvy key from behind the front door of your house ..... and you listened there, in the lobby, behind the door, till a particular quality of silence settled over the stairheid ..... When that special quietness pervaded the stair, you wheeched open the front door, flashed down the stair, opened the lavvy door, got inside and snibbed the door before you could say, "Domestos".

Now, on our landing, in the single-end, between our room-and-kitchen and McCauslin's room-and-kitchen, there lived a young housewife called Madge who had developed the lavvy-going technique until she had made it an art-form! Madge would listen for the silence and got through her door so fast, you thought she hadn't even opened it .... She would pirouette down the stair like a ballet dancer .... aim the key like a rapier at the lavvy door and be inside before you could say, "Toilet paper" ....

But, one night, Madge had listened behind her door .... the special silence had settled .... and her door was opened and she had darted down the stair faster than the speed of light! ..... Key speeding to the lavvy door-lock as if guided by radar .....! Alas, unknown to Madge, big Mrs McCauslin was already in the lavvy .... and had forgotten to snib the door .... Madge pulled the door open with her key .... Mrs McCauslin made a vain lunge to catch the opening door! ..... She missed! .... and went flying out on to the landing to finish spread-eagled with her "St Michaels" round her ankles .....! And then, in one of those glorious examples of Glasgow over-statement, Mrs McCauslin looked up at Madge and said, "There's somebody in ....!"

23

"CAUR FU'!"

Listen. You're on a Glasgow tram .... in the days when Glasgow trams were the finest transport system in the world. This was when you could travel from Milngavie, round the world, past Rouken Glen, and up to the Renfrew Ferry – for tuppence! What a trip on a summer's night!

But you are not on that exotic journey. It's November and your tram is grinding along the Gallowgate from Glasgow Cross. It's cauld and sleety outside .... dark .... and the tram windows are all steamed up .... Listen to this wee cameo as the tram approaches Barrack Street .... The conductress shouts, "Bellgrove!" ..... And the entire complement of that tram – every man, woman and child, turn towards her and in one voice, roar at her, "BARRACK STREET!" The conductress does not flinch. She yells back at them, "Aye, Aw right! Make ma a liar fur wan stoap!"

People resume their individual conversations .... then a drunk man pours himself down the stair from the top deck .... "Ah'm no' steyin' up on that tap deck!" he cries ... "There's nae driver up there! ..." At Bellgrove, one word from the conductress sends him out into the shadows ... "AFF!"

Push your way up to the front of the bottom deck now .... Listen to her with the face like Boris Karloff ..... "In the name o' God, Jane, Ah've been in that Housin' Manager's room that often the wee office lassie thinks we're makin' sweet music together .... Away tae Hell! His face is a' plooks! It looks worse than the fungus growin' on oor back bedroom wa' – an' that's whit Ah wis in complainin' aboot! Says he tae me, 'Mrs

24

McKenna, it's condensation!' An' Ah says tae him, 'Mr Delaware –
condensation my arse!' .....''

Up there – half way along the top deck – her with the fag welded to
her upper lip ..... Listen to her .... "Her an' her man hiv the single-en'
two up. New tae the close. Wan son they hiv. Glaikit lookin'. She talks
like yon ... like Little Red Ridin' Hood. She tellt Gracie next door that
her man wis a pharmacist ..... A pharmacist! then Aw saw him comin'
up the stair wi' cley on his boots! So ah grabbed her by the lapel as she
came oot her door an' Ah says, 'Here, hen. How come your man's a
pharmacist, yet Ah sees him comin' up the stair wi' cley on his boots ..?'
An' she says, 'Well ... he assists on a farm!' Tell me ma heid's made o'
puff candy! Oor parrot fell oot the cage when Ah tellt him that wan!
Three in a single-en' – the boy must sleep in the press at the jawbox ....
Aye, he looks saft. She's been sayin' she's sendin' him tae the bally-
dancin'! The bally-dancin'! The poor boy! Ah'll bet he thinks a leotard is
a lion's shite! Haw! Haw! ....' The fallen cigarette is burning a hole in
her skirt ....

Oh, there, the girl with the Jean Harlow look .... Hear what she's
saying .....

"Naw ..... Ah've had enough o' that followin'-up-picture ... Ah gi'ed
Flash Gordon's photy tae oor Alice. Whit's wrang wi' Flash? Ah canny
stick him any mair. No' efter last week! Ah walked oot the matinee
disgustit wey him! Well, he's in the space-ship starin' oot the windae as
if he wis watchin' for the coalman ..... an' the High Priest is pressin'
buttons an' pullin' levers like mad! the sweat's runnin' aff his moustache
.... Efter a while he turns tae Flash an' says, 'Captain Gordon – I have
managed to change the gravitational co-ordinates – the run-away planet
Zoltar will not now crash into the Earth!.....'

So, big Flash looks at the High Priest an' says, 'That's fine ...' That's
fine!? The auld High Priest has knocked his pan in tae save the world
an' a' this big stookie Flash Gordon can say is, 'That's fine .....' Ah stood
up in the picture hoose an' shouted, 'Ya eejit! Whit size dae *you* take in
miracles!' ..... So Ah did! ...." A wee bit of a debate going on just inside
the bottom deck ..... The buxom lady has just asked for a penny one for
herself and a ha'penny one for her son .....

Hear the conductress. "A ha'penny wan for him!? He's got long
breeks on!" And the woman is saying ....

"If it goes by the length o' the breeks you're wearin' – then, a penny
wan for him an' a ha'penny wan for me!"

The old woman in the shawl has turned round to say, "If it goes by
the length o' the breeks you're wearin' – then Ah should travel for
nothin'!!....."

Now ..... wasn't it? .... The finest transport system in the world ....

IMAGINE THAT

Young apprentice bricklayers like me absorbed much of their education in stinking bothies on wet days when we couldn't get up on the scaffold to lay bricks. We would listen to the patter not only of the rain on the roof, but of the worldly-wise, far-travelled bricklayers squatting round the fire ... Ginger was a philosopher. He deduced that we Scots suffered from what he termed, The Cardboard Tube Syndrome – a kind of always being pipped at the post ..... We pressed him for a clearer explanation of the term, Cardboard Tube Syndrome, and Ginger said, "Well, you know how you can knock your pan in runnin' for a bus – you just get up to it and the conductor pushes you back and says 'Full up – get the next bus!' ..... or you dash into the newsagent's to get your copy o' the 'Wizard' because you're desperate tae read the next instalment o' 'Big Mac' – yon story aboot the cowboy detective – an' the newsagent says, 'Sorry – sold the last wan two minutes ago' ... Or, even mair tae the point, you're in the toilet ... an' you've jist completed a satisfactory evacuation? .. OK? An' you turn tae the toilet roll holder ... an' a' that's there is – the cardboard tube! That's where psychologists got the term – The Cardboard Tube Syndrome. It happens mair tae Scots than any other race under the sun ...."

THE UPS AND DOWNS OF LIFE AND DEATH

Still in that stinking bothy ..... innocent apprentices and fly, old bricklayers ....

Old Storrie recounted so many of the hardships he had to endure working around the world. Building skyscrapers in New York in mid-winter, men were pushed to the *limits* of endurance.

He told us, "I'll never forget workin' oan a scaffold – twinty-two storeys high – jist up frae Times Square. It was so cauld, the birds were flyin' backwards tae keep their eyes frae freezin' up ..... Aye, it was so cauld we had tae wear thick rubber suits for protection ....

Unfortunately, my mate, Casey, accidentally fell off the scaffold – right tae the street below! He bounced for five days! Finally, for humanity's sake ... they shot him doon ..... But they found he had died o' starvation ....." A brooding silence settled over the bothy .... and we young apprentices, staring into the fire, pondered how cruel life could be ....

ELEGY FOR ISA

Take heed o' the looks on great-grandfaithers' faces,
Reflectin' the ploys an' the people an' places
Remembered wi' pain an' wi' pleasure this day
When fugitive tears must be flickered away .....
An' note, as these auld jokers pensively sit,
Their eyes say much mair than their tongues would admit .....
They know why the Calton seems quiet an' dull ....
Why Kent Street is hung wi' a desolate lull .....
Why pale windae-cleaners are bowed in despair .....
An' judges are jaded in Jocelyn Square .....
In sullen Sautmarket .... an' sad Sarryheid .....
Are men who will mourn because Isa is deid ....
They'll think o' a lassie nae man could forget –
Who made kings an' courtiers break oot in sweat .....
They'll whisper o' nights at the back o' Graham's pen'
When Isa turned shiverin' boys intae men .....
Great-grandfaithers see ower the tangle o' years .....
The nights when the gallery rang wi' their cheers .....
The Metropole chorus girls swingin' the chassis .....
An' Isa displayin' why lassies are lassies .....
Time painted her scene on the canvas o' life
In warm-hearted colours o' passion an' strife .....
It shaped her a big, lazy man, for her pains,
A stall at the Barras, an' ten hungry weans .....
It took her tae pawnin' a chair an' a bike
Tae feed the hale stair in the General Strike
Wi' custard an' chips an' a big Belfast ham
That fell aff a lorry right intae her pram!!
Remember her. Dancin' in Waverley Station ..
A mini-skirt granny .... A disco sensation .....
An' screamin' her heid aff for John! Paul! George! Ringo!
An' playin' six cards a' at wance at the bingo .....
Auld Isa ..... Time's brushed the last shades on her scene .....
In Flannigan's Home she was dowager queen .....
Look gently on Isa ... Forbear wi' your sneer ....
Withoot her, a few o' ye might no' be here .....
Noo .... pale windae-cleaners are bowed in despair ....
An' judges are jaded in Jocelyn Square ...
In sullen Sautmarket an' sad Sarryheid
Are men who will mourn because Isa is deid .....

TAM

Tam was the scientist and inventor up our stair. To save the neighbours from the messy chore of stuffing paper, sticks and coal into the back-court wash-house fire to get a boilerful of sudsy, hot washing water, Tam invented a new gas burner fixed to a rubber tube led from his kitchen stove .... The resultant explosion sent the roof of the wash-house on to the bar of a public house two streets away. Thereafter, the neighbours went to the "steamie". The matter was hushed up.

Tam's real forte was radio. Long before the days of C B radio, people like Tam were called radio hams. They spoke to each other from places all round the earth .. Tam's equipment was a tangle of wires and buttons and speakers, but it was effective. His wife, Jean, went out one night to visit her granny ... but she couldn't tell Tam because he was in the middle of a conversation with Bill in Sydney, Australia ....

When Jean came back she discovered she had gone out without her keys, and no amount of battering on the door or shouting up to the kitchen window could attract Tam's attention to her plight of being locked out. He was still talking to Bill in Sydney, Australia.

Desperation stimulated Jean's resourcefulness. She rushed round the corner to Tansy who was another radio ham – not broadcasting at that moment. She explained her difficulty and immediately, Tansy was at his transmitter contacting his radio friend, Pedro, in Rio De Janeiro to tell him about the Jean lock-out.

Pedro then linked up with *his* friend, Ahmed, in Cairo, and asked him if he could get the urgent message through to Sydney, Australia. Ahmed lost no time in transmitting the story of the keyless Jean to his link man, Zeke, in – would you believe? – Sydney, Australia. Zeke's wife ran round to Bill's house, got in, and told Bill to tell Tam his wife Jean was locked out without the keys .... and that Tam had to open the door because Jean would be at it in two shakes of an aerial.

Tam did his "Over-and-out" bit with Bill, and got the door opened just in time for Jean to barge in. He had just started to say "The wonders o' modern science ..." when Jean lifted his transmitter and melted him over the head with it! Just as Tam sank into unconsciousness he was heard to murmur, "Reception wis very good the night ....."

JEAN

One subject was never a favourite topic of conversation in our family – the job our Auntie Jean worked at. It hardly made for respectable chat, it was thought. You see, she was a cleaner in a Glasgow model lodging house. Well. Imagine. Our Auntie Jean among all those flea-bitten old drop-outs stinking with cheap wine and stale sweat .....

Jean was always different from the rest of the family. When my mother was a lassie, she went through a phase of attending every evangelical meeting she could find, and got "saved" at every one of them! One night she got home from a meeting about quarter-past nine when all the family were in bed. (Folk had to rise early for work in those days).

My mother slipped in beside Jean who was turned to the wall in the set-in bed. "Jean", she whispered, "Jean ... I've been saved ....." And Jean snorted, "Well, let them that's no saved get tae sleep!!"

Jean and her pal, Maggie, were the first women ever to smoke in the district – in public! People looked sideways at them and called them "fast" women .... They wore outrageous fashions .... and drank whisky!

They were so fast that no men ever caught them. They remained un-wed. But Jean actually talked two other people into marriage. Peggy the spinster. Bill the bachelor. In their middle years. They lived up Jean's stair for years. And for those years, they never looked at each other – never passed the time of day! They had never been introduced to each other .... Then Jean began the ploy of saying to Peggy that Bill had been asking what kind of woman she was .... Bill never had! And, of course, Jean told Bill that Peggy had been making enquiries about him .... Peggy never had.

That auntie of mine carried the nonsense even further. She told them that each was asking kindly after the other. This led to Peggy and Bill exchanging wee smiles .... And then saying, "Hello" ... "Nice day .." .... "Good evening ...". These overtures were followed by stairhead chats ... Peggy having tea at Bill's .... Bill having supper at Peggy's ... A night out at the pictures ..... Going steady .... Romance bursting into full bloom! Marriage! Jean the matchmaker, sang "The Old Rustic Bridge By The Mill" at their wedding .... And there was the night that a drunk man staggered out of the public toilet at Parkhead Cross .... doubled up in apparent agony! He was shouting, "Ah canny straighten ma back! Ah canny straighten ma back! ..." Rain was battering the pavements as he collapsed into a puddle ....

Passers-by ignored him .... until Jean and Maggie came along. They went right to the man and they were soaked to the skin by the time they dragged him into a close, still moaning that he couldn't straighten up ....

It sounded like a disc problem .... Maggie raced away to phone for an ambulance as Jean took off her coat and put it over the man .... She put her scarf under his head, too .... Jean tried to turn him slightly to loosen his collar and tie .... Maggie was back ... and they could hear the ambulance coming up the Gallowgate .... It was at that moment .... Jean said to Maggie, "I can see how the poor sowl canny straighten his back ..... The daft bugger has buttoned his fly-buttons intae his tap waistcoat buttonholes ....."

Jean always came to visit you un-announced. In the days when the check key was kept in the front door permanently, anybody could turn it and walk in, but the usual thing was to shout, "Are ye in?!" Jean never shouted. Suddenly she was just there .... in the chair by the fire ... and well into a conversation before you gathered your wits enough to know what she was talking about ... ".... an' Ah said tae him, 'Your drawers?! How wid Ah know where your drawers were? Ah didny take them! Ah never wore men's drawers in ma life! An' Ah widny wear yours if Ah wis at the North Pole naked!'.."

The manner of her leaving was just as instant .... You realised the voice had stopped .... turned your head .... and she was gone .... She never said goodbye .... All that showed she had ever been there were the smoke rings from her cigarette still floating up through the washing drying on the kitchen pulleys .... When Jean died, the thoughts of some members of our family turned to the money they were sure she must have left .... Well, working all her life and never spending very much – she must have had it stacked away ...

Jean left nothing. It was then we found out she had been giving most of her money over the years to this poor soul and that poor soul among those stinking drop-outs in the model lodging house .... They came to her funeral in the shirts and jackets and boots she had bought for them ....

Surely all the trumpets sounded for Jean on the Other Side ... If they didn't, then the Heavenly Musicians' Union have a sin to answer for .....

THE SONG-WRITER

On occasion, my grandfather would come swaying up the stair to his top-flat house, singing a cheeky parody on that grand old Scottish song, "The Auld Hoose". He would sing, "The auld hoose .... the auld hoose .... although the rooms are bare .... I'd rather hiv the auld hoose .... than Wellwood's doon the stair ...." The Wellwoods were our good neighbours who lived just below us ....

Now, that song, "The Auld Hoose", is one of those songs many of us grew up with .... thinking that it had always been there to be sung .... that, surely, it was even sung in the Garden of Eden ...... like "Bee Baw Babbity" ..... or "Hickory, Dickory, Dock". My mother used to sing songs like that .... Songs like "The Rowan Tree" .... "The Laird o Cockpen" .... "Charlie Is My Darling" .... "Will Ye No' Come Back Again" .... I thought they were "forever" songs ... Years passed before I discovered those songs my mother sang were written by a beautiful lass called Carolina Oliphant, who became known more widely as Lady Nairne.

When I went out on research for the making of a short film on this lovely, multi-talented song-writer, little did I guess how close I would get to this fascinating lady.

Of course, it's well-known that she lived in the Auld Hoose of Gask in Perthshire .... then in the New Hoose .... and admirers called her "The Flower of Strathearn". But it was when I met her descendant, Mr Laurence Blair-Oliphant, that I knew I was becoming surrounded by the perfumes .... the softnesses ... the artistry ... the fun ... the deepness ... of Carolina Oliphant ... the darling of the Jacobite cause ....

At Ardblair Castle near Blairgowrie, Laurence took me to a very special room which seems to have its own quietness ... In that room are all of Lady Nairne's personal and intimate belongings .... Her bed ... her chair ... her combs and brushes ... and a book containing her quite magnificent colour drawings of birds and flowers .... each page protected by soft tissue .... the scent of her was all round me ....

And over in a corner, I sat down at the piano she had used to marry her words to the music .... to make songs that would be woven into Scottish history and culture .....

Then, with one finger, I actually, on that very piano, picked out the tune of "The Auld Hoose" ..... The thought came into my mind then .... What would my grandfather and the Wellwoods have had to say about this ...?

THE LONGIN' ERM O' THE LAW

This polisman fancied big Bella ...
But big Bella jist wisny too willin' ....
He tailed her through back-coorts an' closes –
Just like Kojak oot tailin' a villain ....
Things never went right for this polis –
An' a loat o' folk ca'd him a dope ....
They said that he thought camiknickers
Were jist people who stole scentit soap ....
He wance donned a Romeo costume ....
Serenadin' frae twilight tae dawn ....
Then he offered big Bella this lovebird ....
But the thing did a job on his haun'!
At last, it seemed Bella wis waarmin' ....
For she said tae this cop, "Listen, Joe ....
Some frien's o' mine quite like the polis ....
Ma auntie loved Dixon, you know ....
An' Bergerac sizzled oor Sadie ...
Wance .... the thrill in her stomach wis Starsky ....
But, Ah've goat this feelin' for you, Joe ....
Aye .... you're just a big pain in the arsky ....!"

CITY FOR ALL SEASONS

Hogmanay. Ten minutes to midnight. Ashes long since cleaned from the fire and taken down to the midden. Shortbread ... currant bun ... ginger wine ... bottle of whisky ... on a clean, white tablecloth. All to ensure good luck next year. Time for my father to lift the kitchen window ... the front room window ... to let the New Year in. And he says, "Ah wonder which direction the New Year will come in this year ..... It'll likely come in through Maryhill. It came in frae Baillieston direction last year ...." The bells ring. The works' horns hoot. Ships' sirens squeal all the way up from the Clyde. But it's so noisy. I listen intently. Still I can't pick the direction the year's coming in. My dad says confidently he was right. It was Maryhill. How does he know?

My brother comes to the door late. Should have been in an hour ago. Missed the bus. He's the first-foot. Empty-handed. My mother tells him to go and get something – anything! In a flash he's down the stair and back up again with an empty silk-stocking box out of the midden. He's allowed in as firstfoot. The box is not empty. It's got some ashes in it from the midden. Probably the ashes my mother cleaned from the fire earlier on. That year was just as lucky and unlucky as any other year .....

Easter Monday. Does it always rain? Inevitable picnic to Hogganfield Loch. Sit on wet grass. Eat corned beef sandwiches. Swig lemonade. Row a boat over the loch to the island. Get the boat stuck in the reeds and the mud. Lose sanny stepping into the glaur to re-launch the boat. On the way home, get the red pullover to look like a Partick Thistle jersey by sliding on my back down the yellow clay slope of the Sugarolly Mountains. Sugarolly Mountains? Don't look for them. They're under the M8 now ....

June. Sunday School trip to Saltcoats. Races on South Beach. Tea in tinnies. Tastes the way the seaweed smells. This reminds my mother to speak to my dad. She says, "Noo, Jimmy, don't you dare tell your Saltcoats story in front o' any o' the Sunday School people ...... That wan about the Glasgow Sewage Workers' trip to this town .... And wan o' them gettin' aff the train ... an' faintin' wi' the smell o' fresh air .... An' they could only bring him roon' by throwin' a pail o' – yon stuff – about him .... Don't you dare!" My dad says, "Oh, you mean a pail o' dia–" "DON'T!", she cries, "Here's the Sunday School Superintendent comin'!" My dad tells the man it's a great day and a great place for a trip .... Very popular with Sunday Schools ... old-age pensioners .... and sewage workers .... My mother nips a lump out of his arm ....

Glasgow Fair Friday. The day that has no night. A magic evening at the Carnival on Glasgow Green. What excitement! One of the famous Lindbergh Brothers is up on his eighty-foot high tower. We are quite close to the twelve-foot diameter tank on the ground which is brimming with water. Some kind of spirit is spread on it and it's set ablaze! Lindbergh, high above, has stepped into a sack. He has a lighted torch in his hand. He waits for the breeze to die. He lights the sack .... and he is swallow-diving to the tank like a flaming meteor! SPLASH! He's in the tank. Water and flames fly everywhere. But the flames snuff instantly. Even those that were lighting his hair .... Then one of those daft, incongruous things. There's a scratchy gramophone on a stall playing the worst song I have ever heard ... "Why Do Women Like Them Like Men Like Them, And Why Don't Women Like Me ....." Because of Lindbergh, I'm saddled with that song for life ....

Hallowe'en. The dark spirits must be about. The headmaster has broken the top set of his false teeth biting too hard on the fork at the dooking for apples. Miss Morrison slips on the gym hall floor as she carries in the Hallowe'en cake. On her way to hit the floor, she twists .... which means she takes the treacle scone, hanging on a string beside her, full in the face! Down she goes. Most of the Hallowe'en cake disappears inside her blouse. She retrieves quite a lot. But nobody will eat it. The headmaster has a rare excuse ..... Somebody has choked the lavatory pan with a turnip lantern ...

December. Playing guesses, using the adverts on the fire curtain at the Queen's Theatre in Watson Street. Up goes the curtain on the Christmas pantomime! Sam Murray ..... Frank and Doris Droy ... The script is incendiary! Matrons' ears curl with the heat ... before their girdles burst with their guffaws!

Shame about Dick. He did such a good job organising our works trip to the pantomime. But it was the lads. Some of our lads. For a laugh. They had told an usherette there was a man causing a disturbance in the gents' toilet. Dick is in the toilet. On his lawful occasions. Three bouncers rush in. Grab Dick and throw him out of the side exit into the lane. His braces are left inside. On earth .... peace .... goodwill .... toward men ... Hogmanay. Ten minutes to midnight. Wonder which way the New Year is coming in this year ... Aw, cut the kiddin' .....

"IT'S MY MOTHER'S BIRTHDAY TO-DAY"

Sentimental songs. My goodness, people in the thirties had the taste for them. They added enough sugar to make the times less bitter than they might have been.

The variety theatres offered a bright, glossy, two-hour escape from reality for thruppence, sixpence, ninepence and a shilling – from gallery down to orchestra stalls. There, you could hear the big ballad-singer with the blonde, curly hair, dressed in a white silk suit that looked like Marlene Dietrich's pyjamas. Joe O'Rourke, he was.

One year, for a few months, as the grand finale to his act, Joe was singing a syrupy favourite ... "It's my mother's birthday today ..... I'm on my way .... with this lovely bouquet ......" A verse, a chorus, a repeat chorus .... and then Joe would come down to the edge of the stage ....

the house lights would go up ... and he would say, "Is there a mother in the audience whose birthday is today ...?" If he were dead lucky, there would be, but most times there wasn't. So Joe had to ask for a mother with a birthday this week .... this month ....

Eventually some mother would be coaxed to come down to front stage .... Joe would meet her at the centre aisle ... ask her name ... kiss her ... and present her with a gigantic bouquet of red roses. That kiss sent the audience wild! They roared and danced and cheered till the chandeliers above went into a swing!

It was at a variety show in the Shettleston Public Hall that I got a real close-up of this part of Joe's act. He had sung his verse and two choruses – the house lights were up – and he asked if there was a mother in the audience having her birthday that day. No takers.

Joe went on to ask for a mother who was having her birthday this week. Sure enough, a silver-haired lady in a threadbare coat, sitting quite near me in the back stalls, got up and walked down the centre aisle .... Joe took her hands, asked her name, and she said, "Rita" .... The kiss .... and then the bouquet ....

The audience went mad! They stamped and screamed in joy for the dear old lady. She started back up the aisle towards her seat .... with the slow steps a bride would take coming to her wedding .... The old dear was loving it .... She moved the red bouquet from side to side to let the audience see it .... With her free arm she waved like the Queen Mother .... People were dropping half-crowns and shillings into her pockets .....

It was then that I looked at her companion in the seat along from me. An enormous, fat lady .... shaking like a jelly in heavy traffic ... tears streaming down her face ..... It took a minute for it to dawn on me that she wasn't crying – she was helpless with laughter! When the birthday lady got back to her seat, the two hugged each other in wild, giggling kinks! They became so helpless they slid off their seats on to the floor and a few of us had to oxter them out to the vestibule to recovery. The fat woman was gurgling through her giggles, "Ah'm wettin' masel'!" Out through the front door, the two gulped for cool air .... and they got control of themselves enough for the large one to whisper loudly in my ear ... "The auld bugger ... Her birthday's no' till July .... Her name's Kate – no' Rita ..... She's a spinster .... never had a wean in her life!" Then she slumped onto the front door steps .... speechless in the vibrations of a thunderous belly laugh. The silver-haired birthday lady collapsed on top of her with the bouquet of red roses jammed between them ... and she tittered, "Ah always wantit tae get intae show business ..."

The grave-faced door-keeper growled, "They're talkin' through drink ....."

AMUSING THE MUSE

Scotland has more poets, rhymesters, versifiers, to the acre than any other country under the sun! We are practitioners in the alchemy of words! Scottish dukes, bookies or lavatory attendants can be relied upon, without provocation, suddenly to effuse poetically about a remembered sunset over Kintyre .... or a remembered Kenny Dalglish goal ....

My grandfather was a dabbler in the doggerel. He would come home of an evening in the days when the pubs shut at nine o'clock, suitably fuelled for effusing ... He would pace the kitchen floor and then say to his son who would be sitting by the fire reading Dante ... He would say, "Johnnie ... take this doon." And Johnnie would copy down immortal couplets such as

"The bulls came tearin' oot the wood,
An' did the coos a power o' good ...."

I have since tried again and again to capture that special word-magic conjured by my grandfather .... with efforts such as,

"Don't send your granny tae clean oot the drains –
It canny be good for her varicose veins ...."

Or,

"This bricklayer ate a brick a day ...
He's no' the same at a' noo ....
Indeed, he hisny much tae say ....
Because he is a wa' noo ...."

However, if *you* don't mention them again ... neither shall *I* ...

"G'ON YERSEL', LOTTIE!"

Lottie was born to lose. She came in on the trailing bottom end of the social scale. A wean of the hungry twenties and thirties. One disease of the poor, then, was rickets. An inadequate diet, lacking in Vitamin D, caused the bones to twist grotesquely out of shape. Lottie was a victim. Her legs were so deformed, she had a halting, shambling walk.

After her schooldays, she worked in mills .... in factories ... but she found her niche driving an overhead crane in an engineering works. Lottie handled that crane with the same delicacy of touch that an artist uses with his brush. Her lifting and setting of loads were always inch-perfect. For lads and lassies in the thirties, there was the imperative requirement to display a high degree of efficiency in getting through the quickstep .... modern waltz ... slow-foxtrot ... tango ... rumba ... and so on. You just *had* to be good at the dancing! it was an accomplishment as necessary as being able to read and write! Your popularity was in direct proportion to your ability to "twinkle-toe" it on the shiny floor. Lottie went to the dancing ...... And there was magic abroad in the air ...

Whenever a young fellow took pity on Lottie within ear-shot of the music of Joe Loss at the Playhouse Ballroom ... Billy McGregor at the Barrowland Ballroom .... Louis Freeman at the Albert .... George Elrick at Dennistoun Palais .... whenever a young fellow asked Lottie to dance .... the ugly duckling was transformed into the graceful swan .....!

She floated across the floor, through the most intricate routines, with fairy lightness .... Lottie was a joy to dance with! .... she was kind of ethereal .... it was like dancing with an apparition ....

Her fame spread. Young blokes were asking which hall she'd be at next weekend. They were queueing up to dance with Lottie!

But the glorious night of glorious nights was the warm Saturday in high summer at the local Miners' Welfare Hall. The final of the District Open Ballroom Dancing Championship – Quickstep, tango, modern waltz and slow-foxtrot.

Lottie was magificent ..... responding to the smooth guidance of her partner, Erchie .... No prima ballerina of the Bolshoi ever displayed finer artistry than the poetic movement Lottie dazzled us with that night. She and Erchie won the competition from here to Dreamland and back again! In a class by themselves! And in the glow of victory ... and the acclaim of her pals ... on that starry night ... Lottie even looked beautiful ..... So she had won treasures that would last her into her old age .... I always wished she might have grandweans to tell her stories to ....

History, of course, doesn't remember people like Lottie. But I remember Lottie. Child of Poverty. Disabled Person. Precision Crane-Driver. Queen of the Dance.

REAL LIFE

Transmit this advice, Lord, tae a' would-be weans,
Who hope soon tae sample this Earth's joys an' pains ....
Direct them tae shun scientific creators
Who tinker wi' test-tubes an' strange incubators ....
When intae this life you've a notion for comin' –
Jist try an' make sure that your maw is a wumman!!!

THE VERSATILE GHOST

Filming for Scottish Television's "By the Way" series took me to the old manse at Kinross. It's not a manse now, but it once was, and it replaced an earlier manse on that site. My quest was to find out about the ghost of a minister of that first manse ... and the ghost of his serving-girl who was accused of giving him the colic by putting bats' wings and birds' droppings in his gruel .... When I spoke to the lady of the house, she said, "Och, those ghosts must have been demolished with the first manse. They never trouble us now ..... But we *do* have a most interesting ghost in this house .... Our family are all grown-up .... but sometimes .... in the dark, early hours of the morning, we hear a baby cry .... But there is not a baby within a quarter of a mile of this house ... and the cry seems to come from that front upper bedroom .... And what makes this ghost interesting is what it has to do with the young wives of this town. Because of our common interests, I often invite a group of young wives to this old manse for afternoon tea and a chat. Now, if on the night after one of our meetings, we hear that ghostly baby cry, we know for certain that at least one of those young wives is pregnant!"

What other Scottish ghost could claim to double as a pregnancy test?

SONG OF A TEACHER

What a friend we have in teacher,
She has taught us all we know ....
Now, we're sure to get employment,
Slicing bacon in the Co .....
She has taught us all our tables,
She is surely our best pal .....
I'll invite her for her dinner ...
When I buy the Taj Mahal .....

WE SHALL OVERCOME

It's a wonder that some Lanarkshire towns still survive – towns that nurtured the weavers and the miners and the iron and steel workers ..... Now, those ways of winning bread have gone. But the towns do survive and the folk who live in them now have inherited from their forebears warm hearts for the underdog .... and a hankering to stand with those who are oppressed .....

In a primary school ... in one of those towns ..... it was the time of the day that the five-year-olds loved best. Teacher told them to sit comfortably and she would read them a story ..... They settled in a cosy silence ... The story was "The Three Little Piggies". Teacher told them the three little piggies had decided to build houses for themselves. One little piggy built his house of paper ..... the second built his house of wood ..... and the third little piggy built his house of bricks. There was a perceptible tension growing in the class when the teacher said that the Big Bad Wolf had come along. The childrens eyes widened .... their knuckles whitened ... when they heard that the Big Bad Wolf came to the door of the little piggy who had built his house of paper, and shouted through the door, "Little Piggy! Let me in! Let me in!" Of course, the little piggy shouted back, "No, Mr Wolf, I'll *not* let you in!" Then, teacher said that the Big Bad Wolf shouted through the door, "Little piggy! Let me in – or I'll huff and I'll puff – and I'll *blow* your house down!"

By now the children were on the edges of their seats .... their hands gripped the desks in front of them .... they seemed rigid ... as if afraid to breathe ... Teacher's voice went on .... she said there was a moment of silence behind the little piggy's door and then the brave wee fellow yelled, "No, Mr Wolf, I'll *not* let you in!"

Tension in the class now was almost unbearable as teacher, with just the hint of tremor in her throat, said .... "So, the Big Bad Wolf .... huffed .... and he puffed .... and he *blew* the house down ...!" The thick silence in the classroom ..... seemed then to be endless .... until a little voice near the back of the room ..... said, in its deepest register ..... "The bastard ...!"

THE GRAND OLD SCOTTISH MINSTREL

Some people can waggle their ears .... some can make their knuckles crack .... some can do the splits .... My peculiarity from an early age was writing scraps of daft verse. Now, my father was a dedicated fan of Sir Harry Lauder, and each year about a week or so before Sir Harry's birthday – on the Fourth of August – my dad would have me write a birthday verse or two to the great man .... I did that for years. Indeed, it became such a custom that I kept it on long after my father died – right to the year Lauder died.

Never did I write a piece to the great entertainer without having a letter of appreciation from him – in his own hand. But there came the year when I was summonsed to visit him at Lauder Ha' just on the edge of Strathaven. I felt fine on the bus .... and on the walk from the town centre to the gates of the big house .... but it was when I started to walk up that tree-lined driveway ... the nerves twittered a bit ....

There I was in my good suit ..... shoes polished .... tie straight .... about to meet this man who had become part of Scottish history ..... like Burns ..... Bonnie Prince Charlie ... Jerry Dawson .... Jimmy McGrory ....

Yesterday I was a young fellow laying bricks ... tomorrow I would be a young fellow laying bricks again ... but on this sunny Sunday afternoon in August, I was to be the guest of Sir Harry Lauder .... Round a bend in the driveway ... there was the impressive house built in grey stone ... and there, sitting on his garden seat .... the man recognisable the world over. His greeting to me was, "James! Come awa' an' sit doon beside me, son ...."

Greta, his beloved niece and companion, brought out tea and biscuits .... We talked of many things ..... Scottish verse .... Burns .... the antics of Danny Kaye at Lauder Ha' ..... And we talked about the Glesca "Bursts" which my mother and father had told me about ..... At the turn of the century, heavy drinking had become such a social evil that the Society of Good Templars determined to do something to steer men away from the pubs on Saturday nights. So they organised concerts to run simultaneously in the Landressy Street Hall in Bridgeton, the City Hall in Candleriggs and in the Albion Street Hall ..... Great family entertainment put on by the finest music hall stars of the day! Each performer did a turn at Landressy Street ..... then at the City Hall ..... then at the Albion Street Hall .... and so the shows were all kept running together .....

The evening began with the audience being invited to sing Psalm One Hundred ... "All People That On Earth Do Dwell ....." Then everybody was given a mug of tea and a poke of buns as a pre-show supper ..... Just before the show started, the Chairman invited all present to blow up their empty pokes ..... and on the signal of "One-Two-Three!" they had to burst them all together in one gigantic thunder clap. This device was to prevent anyone bursting a poke during the performance ... That's why the shows became known as the "Bursts" .... Harry Lauder was one of the top team of artistes .....

Benny Lynch had died in the week before my visit to Lauder Ha', and Sir Harry, a devotee of boxing, spoke sadly of the one-time World Flyweight Champion ..... He said to me, "James ... I tried tae help that boy .... but a' Benny would say tae me was, 'Sir Harry ... Ah wis born in the gutter ..... an' Ah'll die in the gutter' ..."

At that time, Hollywood was pre-occupied with making films of famous show-biz folk ..... say like Al Jolson ... James Cagney had just had a roaring success playing the part of George M. Cohan, the American star, in "Yankie Doodle Dandy". Now, Sir Harry always saw George M. Cohan as one of his rivals, but he said that Cagney's performance was brilliant. He said to me, "James, believe me, Cagney's got mair talent than ever George M. Cohan had ...." There was talk about, then, of making a film of Sir Harry's career, so I took the chance to ask him whom he would choose to play him .... There had been mention of a variety of Scottish comedians and singers to do it. But Sir Harry's answer was, "Oh, it would need tae be Cagney tae play me – naw don't bother aboot the accent, son, we'd sort that oot ...." So there!

When Greta left us alone to go and set the evening meal, we talked about his songs ..... where he had sung them .... where I had heard them .... and then suddenly he said to me, "Son, I'm going tae sing you a song I have never sung in public ...." And the rich baritone voice went into a song about a lass in Glendaruel .....

Now, whenever I drive along that road between Strathaven and Galston ..... I remember the summer's day when the man Winston Churchill called "that grand old Scottish minstrel", put on a special performance of a song no other audience had ever heard ..... and I was the audience of one .....

PARENT/TEACHER GET-TOGETHER

Comprehensive school. Big one. Monday morning. Assembly is over and pupils are ensconced in classrooms. Surging through the front door comes a great battleship of a woman. Down the corridor she sails and stops at the chemistry lab. Her big, chubby fist thunders on the door. Nothing happens. Again she has a batter at the door ... In a moment, the door is opened by the wee, shilpit chemistry teacher .....

Without introduction, the large lady bawls at the wee man, "Why did our Arther get wan per cent for chemistry?!" The chemistry teacher raises his eyes to meet those of the mountainous figure towering above him, and without the turning of a hair, replies to the lady, "Madam, I can only conclude he was cheating ....!"

THEY WERE THE PEOPLE

Old Firm supporters have always been good for an anthropological study. Dogs and horses, they say, are loyal creatures. They look positively traitorous compared with Old Firm fans. Take Lenny. His utter devotion to Ibrox was heart-warming ..... if puzzling ....

Lenny would say that it was on a par with an orgasm to stand on the terracing at that moment when the stars in Light Blue came on to the field before the game .... He would say ... "Ma ears are filled wi' the sounds o' the Ibrox faithful ..... An' a' ma eyes can see is a blue blur ....."

We would ask Lenny. "Whit kinda gemme did Davie Meiklejohn hiv the day ... Lenny would answer, "He played a binder! A veritable binder!...." Davie Meiklejohn had, at that time, been retired for twenty years .... !

Crannie was to Celtic what Lenny was to Rangers. He could have lived happily on the grass mowings from Celtic Park. But legend had it that Crannie's devotion to the Bhoys reached such a quality of selflessness, that the Celtic Board decided on a course of action never taken before and certainly never taken since. They actually allowed Crannie, during home games, to run up and down the running track behind the linesman!

Those were the days of the legendary Jimmy Delaney. Crannie always chose to be on Jimmy's side of the field .... And whenever Jimmy picked up a ball on the midfield line .... and went speeding down the right wing to cross one of those magic hanging balls in towards goal ... Crannie would race after him down the track! On a very wet and muddy day at Celtic Park ..... Delaney – halfway through the second half – had caught the ball almost on the touchline and away he flashed down the right wing ..... Crannie went to go after him! Slipped in a puddle. Fell on his face ..... But raised his head and shouted, "Carry on, Jimmy! Don't wait for me!...."

"GET TAE – !"

Maist sensible people you blether among,
Will tell you the trouble wi' weans is – they're young!
But worldy-wise adults dae nothin' aboot it,
For, sooner or later, weans tend to grow oot it!
Before they *dae*, though, you watch bedlam break loose!
They eat mounds o' grub an' tramp mud through the hoose!
Play tig wi' tomatoes – drive neebors insane ......!
My! don't you jist wish you could be wan again ...!!

SONG OF THE HIPPODILE

Verse:
As I wandered through a lonely, shady glade,
By a quiet little pool of marmalade,
From a ping-pong tree, I heard this an-i-mal
Say that no one ever wants to be her pal ...
I could feel my wellies filling with despair,
As I heard this little hippodile declare ....
Chorus:
I'm a little hippodile,
And I always try to smile ....
Oh, please, do not be afraid, or make a fuss ....
If you're scared of little me,
Well, it could be worse, you see,
For I might have been a crocopotamus!

"IN THE IMAGE OF GOD, EH?"

"Excuse me", said the lad in purple boots,
"But, did ye spot – Ah'm here – an' breathin' ..... Naw?
It's jist that, these days .... well .... Ah hiv ma doots .....
Ah wondered if ye noticed me at a' .....
They said it wid be rerr at seventeen –
Then's when they a' stop takin' ye for grantit .....
It's really *no'* that wey ..... know whit Ah mean?
D'ye ever get the feelin' you're no' waantit.....?
When Ah wis young, ma granny did the urgin' –
'Son, learn your nouns an' square roots', she wid fuss .....
She thought Ah could become a great brain surgeon –
Or maybe even drive a Sixty bus ....
Yon dear auld wrinkled face said no' tae dither –
Grab 'a the school can gi'e – that's how tae win! ....
They taught me how a' this world fits thegither .....
But ..... noo Ah canny find where *AH* fit in .....
Big Danny says we shouldny get annoyed –
The set-up noo is jist for thieves an' gluttons ....
We're – scenery – no' meant tae be employed ....
But Danny's heid is full o' magic buttons ....
'You're made like God!' you'll hear ma granny say,
'He's no' redundant – *your* turn must be due!'
Ur we God's image? – even Danny tae .....?
Ma granny said it ..... so it must be true ....."

THERE WAS A LAD .....

Burns Suppers break up the long, dreich, wearying wintertime that seems dreicher as it starts just after the gulping and gorging of the New Year Festivities. Spring seems light years away, and the Burns Supper is the bright space station we stop off at for re-fuelling. But it's not true, as some cynics say, that if you've been to one Burns Supper, you've been to them all. They come in a variety of styles.

I, once, had to deliver the Address to the Haggis at a Burns Supper organised by a group who will want to coorie under their cloak of anonimity. You see, despite mad car trips and desperate, screaming phone calls, the organisers could not contact the butcher who was supposed to have delivered a load of haggis! He had let them down! Right up to minutes before the great Supper was due to begin, not one single haggis could be laid hand on!

It was one of those crises which requires the barrel of human resourcefulness to be scraped until its bottom is clean .....! There were murmurings among the assembled Supperites as the start time was delayed by five minutes ... ten minutes ... fifteen .....

Then flash! the big grocer on the committee suddenly went rushing towards his car and shouting to his mate, "Come oan wi' me!" They returned in no time laden with three or four dozen tins of haggis from the grocer shop!

The feast was on! But, obviously, to preserve the ceremony, I was required to effect a quick paraphrasing of the Bard's eulogy on the pudding ..... The tin of haggis was piped in ..... the assembly clapped in time to the music ..... Plate and tin were placed before me. I lifted the accompanying tin-opener and said something like ...

"Fair fa' the honest shinin' tin
Technology has stuffed you in ....."

Incidentally, the tinned haggis was a joy to the palate .....

THAT MAN TAE MAN THE WARLD O'ER .....

Oil men came gushing into a Burns Supper I had the pleasure to attend in the North East. At the pre-Supper gathering I seemed to be surrounded by ten-foot-tall Texans. I got the job of trying to make conversation with one who could have been a stand-in for Gary Cooper.

Desperately grabbing at something to say, I said, "Hiram ..... What is your assessment of Burns ..?" Hiram looked at me. Rubbed his chin, then said in his Texan drawl, "Well ..... I reckon he was never the same after he lost Gracie Allen ...."

THE SOUNDS OF AYR

As the years offered me more and more joyous visits to Ayr, I discovered that the sounds that have come echoing through this honest town, have not been confined to the roars of punters yelling at the favourite – "Stay there ya beauty!!!" Legend has it that maybe Old King Cole came through with his fiddlers ..... Certainly the Romans did ..... and the great Scottish patriot ... Wallace ... the Covenanters ... and the poet of humanity ....

Auld Ayr ... the wind has heard your music ...
It's heard the sang your sea-birds sing ....
It's heard the chants o' Roman legions ....
An' themes o' hope your Kirk bells ring ....
Auld Ayr .... the wind has ay been singing'
Defiant songs that Wallace sang .....
Your Covenanters' psalms o' glory .....
That, ower the strife, tae Heaven rang .....
Auld Ayr ..... the wind has caught the echo
O' words that lift ... high as the dove .....
Your poet's words in tunes o' freedom .....
His words in melodies o' love .....
Auld Ayr ..... the wind has heard your music ...
That tells the world o' richts an' wrangs ...
For time, nae shorter than forever,
Auld Ayr .... the wind will sing your sangs ....

HEAR THIS

Is this the age when people are not really listening to each other? Funny, too, how some folk can get quite het up about what they think they have heard ... when they haven't really been listening with both ears.

I had done a piece about auld wives' tales in the BBC Radio Scotland programme, "Good Morning, Scotland". In it, I recalled a story my granny once told us. She said that when she was a young girl, there was a pregnant woman in her village who had gone for an evening to a visiting circus. There, the poor lady had been frightened by a bear, and in due course, her baby was born with bare feet .....

A few days after the broadcast, my producer phoned me to read me a letter he had just received from "Anonymous", Dumbarton. The writer demanded a severe reprimand, if not life imprisonment, for the disgusting person who had broadcast the obscene notion that a woman had been made pregnant by a bear!

The producer said to me, "Steady. Do bear up...."

THE ILL-STARRED QUEEN

No other royal figure of Scottish history has taken my imagination in the way Queen Mary has done. Every now and again the Queen of Scots drifts into my thoughts ..... And when I was filming part of her story for Scottish Television's "By The Way" series .... on Castle Island in the middle of Loch Leven ... I came to feel that a moment would come when, turning a corner of the old ruined keep, I might be face to face with the vision of the tall, sad, beautiful queen ..... In that old castle, she spent her last imprisonment in Scotland ..... and made her breath-taking escape ..... But could she ever really escape? Was this her innermost feeling? In fancy ... I could hear her voice .....

Coming across the still waters of the loch ... and reaching over by the shore at Kinross ...

Fareweel tae yon toon by Loch Leven ....
Tae its vennels an' wynds, I've looked ower ...
Tae guess if a whisper drifts roon' them
That wad comfort this Queen in her tower ....
Fareweel tae the slopes o' the Lomonds,
Whaur wi' joy, at the hunt, we have played ....
An' fareweel tae Serf's lonely island ...
Whaur, lang syne, have the quiet men prayed ...
Is this tae be freedom I'm winnin'..?
Is there majesty I can regain ...?
Then why does my hert want tae tell me
That the future is daurkness an' pain ...?
Noo, safely, I'm oot ower the water ...
An' yet, somethin' that hings in the air
Compels me look back on Loch Leven .....
An' tae whisper, "I'll see ye nae mair ....."

MIDGE MUSINGS

Ah'll bet yese never heard o' Clan Chironomidae, did yese?
Well, that's the noble name that science plantit on us midges,
An' though yese might regard us as the lowest form o' life,
Incredibly, within oor tribe, the class-distinction's rife!

Beside a sign in Holyrood that read: "Keep Aff The Grass",
Ah met yon kind o' lassie-midge that nae male-midge could pass .....
Right aff, I hooted, "Doll, let's hiv a bite an' make the scene" ....
Tae which, she answered through her teeth, "Get back tae Glesca
      Green!"

But us yins, jist like Dracula, tae quench oor thirst for thrills ...
Explore the human body .... doon its valleys .... up its hills ...
There's them among ma kith an' kin quite fussy who they bite –
Oor Magnus swore he'd hiv tae get a duchess or a knight!

The day he met the dowager, he knew his time had come –
Right through her corsetry he went, tae bite her on the bum!
He never did get oot again tae savour his elation .....
Caught in a sudden gust o' win', he died o' suffocation!

But really, level-heided midges try tae help the nation,
Though diff'rent schools o' thought insist oor work can cause inflation!
Oor Hector went industrial an' bit an engineer –
Ah'm certain that's the only rise the fella got a' year!

A' midges praise the work the Scottish Tourist Board hiv din,
Wi' bringin' tourists here wi' sich variety o' skin.
They bring their travel-weary flesh tae Scotland's shores, an' dump it –
Whitever colour it may be – we like it an' we lump it!!

THE SHOE

"....... The dug's away tae Hamilton tae buy a new bell .." That's what the old Glasgow back-court song says. Well, when we followed the route of Mary's flight from Loch Leven, with our camera, we reached Hamilton, but never a dog did we see buying a bell. However, something out-of-the-ordinary did happen.

Queen Mary came to stay with her good friends, the great Hamilton family, and was welcomed to safety and rest in Cadzow Castle on the edge of the town and high above the Avon Gorge. In Hamilton Museum, I was discussing with the curator, Mr McKenzie, the story linked to her visit to Cadzow Castle. In the frantic rush from Loch Leven, the Queen had broken one of her shoes, and this shoe was sent down to the Hamilton shoemaker to be repaired. But, of course, Mary's stay at Cadzow Castle was short, because she had to ride out with what army she could gather around her, to face the forces of the Earl of Moray ..... At Langside ..... The world knows of the bitter defeat that sent her fleeing for her life. She was never to return again to Hamilton to slip her queenly toes in to the repaired shoe .....

As we talked, suddenly, Mr McKenzie said, "I've got that shoe here in the Museum .."

I couldn't belive my ears! But, the good man produced a cardboard box from a store (the shoe is not on display) and there in the box was a long, slim black shoe with a fairly high heel – certainly a shoe of the size and style to suit the stature of Queen Mary ....

Local lore has it that the shoe was handed on down the centuries ..... and here it was in Hamilton Museum ..... Was this actually the shoe of the Queen of Scots? Nobody can say yea or nay to that question ..... But Mr McKenzie allowed me to take it ..... so that we could film its return to Cadzow Castle ..... As I stood in the ruins of that Hamilton stronghold, holding this ancient piece of footwear ..... somehow, I felt it really had been there more than four hundred years before ..... Were the shades of those who were there in the hours before Langside, looking on ...?

Could I have said, "Madam, I have returned your shoe ...." ....?

THE CLEARANCES

In so many places, out to the west and up to the north of the country, I've felt it around me. The invisible cloud of sadness over tumbled cottages and long grass growing now at nobody's bidding ..... Croft people lived and worked in those places until their landlords knew that sheep and forests could be more profitable than people. The sending of the people away across the Atlantic to the New World has been given the clean, clinical name of The Clearances ..... That cloud of sadness ..... the wind never blows it away .. the rain never washes it into the river ..... the sun never burns it out .....

But, it was on a misty morning that I felt it so strongly as I came through a village that lost its people ..... The village of Sannox ... on the Isle of Arran .... I thought I heard the voice of the Clearances .....

MIST ON THE MORNING SUN

Mist on the morning sun .....
Mist on the places we would see no more .....
Tears that were shed in days when the heart was sore .....
These were the mist on the morning sun .....

Hills that were sweet with spring .....
Time made those hills our own, from long ago .....
We would not walk again in their winter snow .....
Farewell, our hills that were sweet with spring .....

Only the wind would sing
Round by the gables where the children played .....
Chimneys grew cold, and we saw our peat smoke fade .....
Here was where only the wind would sing .....

Softly, they took our land –
Land that our children's children were to keep .....
Sown for a harvest they would not let us reap .....
Softly, but surely, they took our land .....

Now, we would look away .....
Past where the sun comes down to touch the sea .....
Look to distant time and space where hope would be .....
Now, we were turning to look away .....

Our seed would grow again .....
Somewhere, our God would give us soil to break .....
We were the people this God would not forsake .....
Saying that our seed would grow again .....

Mist on the morning sun .....
Mist on the places we would see no more .....
Tears that were shed in days when the heart was sore .....
These were the mist on the morning sun .....

MAGGIE AND DAN

What a bonus it was for tenement-dwellers if they got folk living up their stair like Maggie and Dan who lived up our stair. They were the joys! Neither of them was aware of it, but in the hard, bitter times up the stair, they took the edge off the pain. And in the cheery times, they were the gilt on the gingerbread.

You see, as God made them, He matched them. Each had the gift of leaving Mrs Malaprop away out of sight ..... Maggie railed on one time, about her brother in trouble with the police. Served him right. Maggie said he was arrested on the football supporters' bus for using "unseen" language ..... And when Woolworth's introduced the system of letting customers choose their own sweets from umpteen varieties massed on the counter, Maggie said, "It's great! They let you pick them at 'ransom' ...." For Dan, the strain of being a shop-steward upset his nerves .... He reported to us that doctor had put him on "tantalisers".

When eventually they could afford a package holiday to Spain, what a time they had! Dancing paellas and eating flamencoes ...! Dan came back saying, "Ah'm that gled we took oor 'haemorrhoid' camera ..." Then he added, "We took piles o' pictures ..." Maggie mentioned meeting a very nice Frenchman ... She never spoke to the man. The language barrier reduced their exchanges to smiles. But she said to me, "He was a French plumber .." I said, "How did you know?" Maggie winked and said, "Well, he had 'bidet' eyes!" Then she hit me a slap on the backside!

THOUGHT ON RAVENSCRAIG

Computer analysis .... coke ovens .... sinter ....
Blast furnaces tappin' through summer an' winter ....
Torpedoes ... an' oxygen .... lime ... an' blue glesses ...
An' ingots ... an' soakin' pits ... strip mills an' presses .....
Pyrometers, panels an' print-oots reveal
A complex technology turnin' oot steel ....!
A' useless, of coorse, withoot Willie an' Tony ....
Chipped mugs o' stewed tea .... an' canteen macaroni .....

END PIECE

Oor city's kind o' magic,
The thinkin' punter quests .....
Where cynics jist see dust-bins,
Wise folk see treasure chests .....

Glossary

Ah.	First person singular.
Ah'll.	Statement of intention: I will/shall.
Ah'm.	Indication of existence: I am.
A kennin' wrang.	Slightly off the straight and narrow.
Awfy.	Glasgow essence of awful.
Bee Baw Babbity.	Ancient musical game. Derived from mazurka. Forerunner of Slosh.
Boax.	Container, made in a number of shapes and a range of materials.
Bothy.	Workmen's hut; strewn with racing sections of newspapers, Page Three cut-outs; poorly ventilated, un-hygenic.
Breeks.	Pants (apparel, not breath).
Cerd.	Prounounced with a hard 'C'. Piece of printed cardboard bearing greetings, instructions, names and addresses, threats of legal action, *etc*. Also one who is a bit of a 'Jack-The-Lad'.
Chantie.	Chamber-pot. Po of character.
Check key.	Simple metal device for allowing access at any door up tenement stair. Its use was mostly happy, but sometimes disconcerting.
Closet.	Peculiarly, in the West of Scotland, a lavatory.
Coo.	Female of bovine species.
Cuddy.	Unremarkable horse.
Cupla.	A pair; brace; two.
Dae.	Do.
Daurk.	Total absence of illumination.
Diz.	Does.
Doots.	Misgivings.
Eejit.	Person of pathologically foolish behaviour.
Erm.	Limb connecting shoulder to hand.
Faur.	A great distance away.
Feart.	Apprehensive.
Fella.	Almost any type of male, from baker's-boy to brain surgeon.
Followin'-up picture.	Cinematographic serial.
Fumin'.	Extremely angry.
Fur.	For: with West of Scotland enrichment of vowel sound.
Gemme.	Sounded with hard "g", but no value given to final "e". A contest with scores accumulated by opposing sides. Quite like a game.
Get.	Person displaying not the slightest indication of being civilised.
Glaur.	Mud with extremely high adhesive properties.

70

Goat.	Past tense of get in the sense of acquiring.
G'on.	First word in a shout of encouragement, inducement or dismissal.
Gonny.	Going to.
Habble.	Crisis of finance or relationships.
Haud.	To keep to; to hold.
Hauf.	Fifty per cent of whole. Usually refers to a measure of whisky.
Heavy.	Beer of a substantial gravity.
Hen.	Affectionate name given to a female of any age or rank.
Hiv.	Have.
Hoarse.	Not a medical condition, but any equine animal from the steeplechaser to the hobby type.
Jawbox.	Ancient metal forerunner of the stainless steel sink unit.
Lavvy.	Affectionate diminutive of lavatory, particularly of stairhead variety.
Loack.	Security device, or the action of using such a device. Also a tress of hair.
Lum.	Chimney.
Maw.	Mother.
Meanjie sod.	Extremely unsavoury person of a miserly disposition.
Naw.	The negative.
Neebors.	People, families, etc, living in close proximity.
Nuts.	Small pieces of coal, also known as churly bits.
Oan.	Sounds proprietorial, but is merely the English preposition, 'on', enriched by a West of Scotland vowel sound.
Oxter.	Cul-de-sac formed by the junction of the arm and shoulder. Armpit.
Photy.	Photograph.
Pipecley.	Slab of chalk-like substance used to produce whitish designs on stairs, closes, etc, which have been newly washed.
Plook.	Boil; usually a facial blemish of a variety of textures and colours.
Ploy.	Devious undertaking.
Po.	Chamber-pot; usually lacking the personality of a chantie.
Polis.	Guardian of law and order.
Pulley.	Light timber frame suspended by ropes from the kitchen ceiling and used for drying the family washing.
Pun'.	Not a play of words, but sixteen ounces.

Rerr.	Not just indicating scarcity as in the English word, 'rare', but having the added Glasgow qualification of indicating what is most enjoyable.
Sannies.	Type of footwear which came as a boon and a blessing after generations of childhood barefootedness. Had ribbed soles and canvas uppers. Worn on trips and picnics and for climbing onto the roofs of backcourt wash-houses.
Single-en'.	Single apartment house in a tenement. Often occupied by more than one person. All human activity was undertaken within its confines. One could wash one's face and fry sausages without getting out of bed.
Skelp.	Slap – usually delivered by hand to face or backside.
Snib.	Bolt.
Snotter.	Mucous effusion from the nostrils.
Sook.	A sharp intake of air or liquid through puckered lips. Otherwise, an obsequious person.
Staur.	Celestial body.
Steamie.	Communal clothes-washing establishment; a forum for oracles.
Stoap.	Stop, with the ehancement of the long, rounded Glasgow vowel sound.
Stookie.	Plaster based on gypsum which is quick-setting. Also a tailor's dummy. Person with as much personality as a tailor's dummy.
Sugarolly.	Rich dark brown liquid brewed from liquorice.
Tearin'.	Moving at high speed without complete regard for safety.
Tellt.	Told.
Thruppence.	3d. Equal to 1·25 New Pence.
Tig.	Chase game in which pursuer catches quarry with a hand-slap.
Tottie.	Potato.
Toty.	Diminutive.
Tupp'ny wan.	Heavy blow delivered with the clenched fist.
Waantit.	Required . . . desired.
Wan.	One.
Wean.	Child.
Wheech.	To throw with a looping arm action. 'ch' sounded as in Scottish 'loch'.
Windae.	Window.
Wis.	Past tense of 'is'.
Yese.	Plural 'you'. This overcomes the lack of a plural 'you' in English and is marvellously comprehensive.